Bushcraft Survival Guide

A Bushcraft Essentials Book to Wilderness Survival Plus Basic Tools, Outdoor Skills and Life Hacks to Get You Through Each Day

By

Zach Parham

Copyright © 2021 – Zach Parham

All rights reserved

No part of this publication may be reproduced, distributed, or transmitted in any form or by any means, including photocopying, recording, or other electronic or mechanical methods, without the prior written permission of the publisher, except in the case of brief quotations embodied in reviews and certain other non-commercial uses permitted by copyright law.

Disclaimer

This publication is designed to provide competent and reliable information regarding the subject matter covered. However, the views expressed in this publication are those of the author alone, and should not be taken as expert instruction or professional advice. The reader is responsible for his or her own actions.

The author hereby disclaims any responsibility or liability whatsoever that is incurred from the use or application of the contents of this publication by the purchaser or reader. The purchaser or reader is hereby responsible for his or her own actions.

Table of Contents

Introduction 6

Chapter 1 7

Essentials of Bushcraft Survival 7

    What is Bushcraft? 7

    Bushcraft Vs. Camping – Know the Difference 7

    Where to Practice Bushcraft and Wilderness Survival? 9

    Developing a Survival Mindset 17

Chapter 2 21

Bushcraft Survival Tips and Tricks 21

Chapter 3 26

Gearing Up 26

    The 5 C's of Survival 26

    Bushcraft Camping Equipment 33

        Shelter and Sleeping Kit 33
        Carrying Kit 34
        Cooking and Water 35
        Personal Hygiene 36

Clothing 37
Other important equipment or tools 39
Chapter 4 44

Surviving In The Bush 44

Building a Shelter for Warmth 44

Find a Suitable Site 44
Check Your Needs 44
Know Your Type of Shelter 45
Navigating and Traveling In The Wilderness 58

Getting Lost and Found 58
Utilizing the Sun to Tell Time and Direction 60
Added Direction Tips 61
Finding, Cooking, and Preserving Food 66

Finding Food 67
Cooking Food 75
Preserving Food 80
Finding, Filtering, and Disinfecting Water 86

Finding Water 86
Filtering Methods 95
Disinfecting Water 99
Making a Fire 102

Things That Bite, Maul, Sting, or Make You Sick 106

Wilderness First Aid Basics 110

Tying Basic Survival Knots 113

Chapter 5 125

Wilderness Survival Mistakes to Avoid 125

Conclusion 136

Introduction

Bushcraft can be traced to Australia (regarded as a bush country), which required that certain skills and knowledge be applied to survive in the wild. However, bushcraft was made popular in the Northern and Southern Hemisphere by Mors Kochanski and Les Hiddins. Today, bushcraft has spread far and wide and is being practiced in different countries of the world.

The term "**bushcraft**" is a commonly discussed subject with different views and opinions. Nonetheless, the act of traveling into the woods and surviving under unfavorable conditions can be referred to as bushcraft. In general, bushcraft involves the application of specialized skills and abilities to survive in any outdoor situation.

Without further ado, let's take a deep dive into what bushcraft really entails and how you can survive in the wild, even in the most unfavorable circumstances that you may find yourself in.

Chapter 1

Essentials of Bushcraft Survival

What is Bushcraft?

In bushcraft, the knowledge you acquire upon completing the pages of this book and putting it to practice in a bushcraft-simulated environment will come in handy when navigating unfamiliar terrain. Although acquiring bushcraft knowledge may take some time, learning it will give you the much-needed outdoor skills and life-hacks to survive in the wild, which will be discussed in this book's subsequent chapters. But before then, let's separate the meaning of bushcraft from camping so that you don't mix up the meaning of these terms.

Bushcraft Vs. Camping – Know the Difference

Camping

This recreational activity includes staying all through the night or some weeks at assigned camping areas. Most times, people hit the camping grounds with their family members and friends to get some time out and inhale natural air.

Camping is not for everyone because not all individuals can choose to sleep on a cold hard floor or a sleeping bag. It is an engaging activity that allows you to meet new people and interact with people from afar.

In camping, you can go with many items and materials that will make your stay enjoyable and exciting.

Bushcraft

Right off the bat, bushcraft is the most challenging because tough survival skills are required than camping. Ordinarily, bushcraft trips are burdening on the body and mind because bushcraft involves staying and surviving unsupervised in the wild, and sometimes, with almost nothing on you. In bushcraft, there is always something to improve upon continually, e.g., your skills. The excitement of "what you don't know" and "what you can achieve" while in the bush is what interests people to engage in bushcraft. It also allows you to disconnect from real-life society and understand what nature is all about.

The two activities (bushcraft and camping) have remarkable similarities because they are both outdoor activities that occur in distant territories. Camping is what everybody can participate in regardless of their abilities to survive. On the other hand, bushcraft requires a learned skillset and some amount of experience to thrive.

Where to Practice Bushcraft and Wilderness Survival?

Like you have with other crafts, bushcraft also entails consistent practice to fully understand and develop your skills. When you practice bushcraft, you gradually build your skills, and eventually, it becomes part of your daily routine.

Bushcraft skills have the potential of saving your life and making you avoid death. But where can one practice bushcraft and wilderness survival to master this much-talked skill?

Bushcraft skills can be consistently practiced on camping trips, in your backyard, on hiking trails, and in your place of work. As you can see, bushcraft skills can be practiced in various places, including where you work.

Meanwhile, before we critically look at where bushcraft and wilderness survival skills can be practiced, you need to know the type of skills that can be added to your skillset.

Type of Bushcraft and Wilderness Skills

Bushcraft and wilderness skills can be divided into sections that is cut across different wilderness survival, such as food, water, shelter, and fire.

- **Locating food in the wilderness:** This is a part of bushcraft and wilderness that needs consistent practice. There are tons of ways to find food in different kinds of wildlife, including hunting, fishing, and foraging.

- **Making of fire:** Fire making is also another vital skill that every survivalist or woodsman should learn. It is a skill that needs the understanding of different ways to make fire and with consistent practice. Cooking is not only the reason why fire is made, but it also makes woodsmen warm when the weather is cold. Hence, it would be best if you strived to learn how to make fire, especially for adverse or unforeseen circumstances.

- **Building shelter:** Making shelter is a skill that needs practice because there are multiple ways of creating one. It won't be advisable to know only how to make fire out of pine branches. This is because you may end up in a wilderness where there isn't one, and you won't know the next step to take. Therefore, learning how to build different types of shelters is an excellent skill that must be learned.

- **Finding water:** Perhaps, this should be one of the most challenging tasks and essential tasks that must be done to survive. Without water, we will become dehydrated and unable to even move further in the wilderness. Not only do you have to find water, but you also need to learn how to purify it and make it safe to drink.

Although these are the major categories where bushcraft and wilderness survival are placed in groups; however, some other skills concern all works of life. Some of which may include awareness skills, knife skills, tool-making skills, navigation skills, and re-purposing skills.

Places to practice bushcraft and wilderness survival

1. **Weekend camping**

This is undoubtedly one of the common places where bushcraft and wilderness survival skills are practiced. With weekend camping, you have the benefit of fantastic outdoor locations and enough time to focus on practicing different bushcraft skills and attempting a few new ones as well.

Check out a few recommended bushcraft skills you can attempt on camping trips:

- **Knot tying:** When building up a camp, attempt more knots and check how functional and non-functional they can be in a few places for protecting your tent.
- **Foraging skills:** Try to discover things such as food
- Making shelter
- **Knife skills:** In here, you can use multiple natural materials to sharpen knives.
- **Fishing skills:** Assuming the camping location permits it, you can practice how to fish. Attempt to create your fishing item from natural materials around you.

2. **Hiking trails**

Hiking trails are a perfect outdoor activity that can give you the chance to practice numerous bushcraft and wilderness skills. Furthermore, it is also an ideal way to engage in family time and encouraging them to learn alongside you.

It would be great to try making several trails in a month because it would massively boost your skills. More options include joining or signing up for a local hiking club, which allows you to know some hiking places that the public can and cannot visit.

In fact, it also offers you the opportunity to broaden your knowledge and meet other experienced hikers.

Bushcraft survival skills on hiking trails include:

- **Making fire:** You can practice the making of fire if it is permitted.
- **Building shelter:** This is yet another amazing skill that can be tried out in a hiking trail. Even if you are not permitted to build a shelter, try to look out for the materials needed to create one.
- **Navigation:** You may not be lost while practicing on a hiking trail, but it is a perfect opportunity to try out several navigating methods. The benefit of trying this out is that you know how to check your location.

- **Finding water:** A skill that enables you to locate water and purify them if possible.
- **Foraging:** This is not only how to locate food in the wilderness, but it is also a way of finding additional natural items that are important. You can go with a few books about local plants and check to know the plants and trees that are useful and serve as food.

3. **Backyard**

Your backyard is the location where you can attempt several skill methods. It is also the perfect place where you can try learning new skills and building on the ones you already know.

Experiment, explore and practice the below skills in your backyard:

- **Foraging:** Practice the skill of searching for food and other vital items and materials.
- **Hunting tools:** Try practicing how to make essential hunting tools like sticks, arrows, and catapult in your backyard.

- **Making fire:** Although making a fire in your backyard is risky, it is also a good location to practice the making of fire.
- **Outdoor cooking:** While in the wilderness, some situations require you to prepare something to eat. So, in your backyard, you can attempt making something of natural items you may typically come across in the wild.
- **Trapping:** This skill can be practiced in your backyard, especially if you have rodents around. Practice or test out your trapping skills by setting traps in your backyard.

Other places to practice bushcraft and wilderness survival include:

- **During driving:** You can practice awareness skills to ensure alertness to the happenings in your environment.
- You can easily practice some knot-tying skills when you have a coffee or lunch break in your everyday job.
- **While waiting in a line:** One can also practice knot tying while waiting in line by reading a knot-tying book. Here is a good one for you https://www.amazon.com/dp/B08VLMR1VT

Bushcraft and wilderness survival entails adapting to circumstances and learning new skills to prepare you for the worst situations. Making out time to practice the skills requires you to devote sufficient time and work to them. However, in some situations, you will have to use your intuition to get the best out of a bad situation, thereby improving your bushcraft skills.

Developing a Survival Mindset

Surviving in a bushcraft situation is not child's play. In fact, you need to have the best level of mindset to come out of a bushcraft survival situation alive, happy, and kicking. But what does developing a survival mindset entails?

A survival mindset in a bushcraft scenario means being aware of what is going on and knowing that you cannot stop or quit even when the going gets tough. With a survival mindset, you are determined to keep on going no matter the bad circumstance at hand. Sadly, not all hikers or outdoor tourists have this survival mindset in them.

It takes hard work, determination, persistence, and patience to survive in the wild, and all these are products of having the right survival mindset.

So, what are the ways to develop a survival mindset?

1. Deal with fear

A fearful person cannot survive or pull through in a bad situation. Fear can even lead to death or injury. It is a brain mechanism that passes a piece of information to your body to halt whatever you are doing because it may lead to injury.

In fact, fear is something that has led to people refusing to have this bushcraft experience. To survive in the wild, you must ensure you deal with all manner of fear.

2. Control your emotions

Allowing your emotions to take over you is the quickest way to cause harm to yourself, physically and mentally. You won't be able to think well if you are unable to control your emotions.

In a bushcraft situation, you need to shun your emotions to survive so as not to get injured or killed.

3. Have realistic goals

In a survival situation, you should have goals you are sure you can meet up with. For instance, you may decide to find food before the day runs out. While doing this, you are sure you won't rest or relax until you have accomplished what you have set out to achieve.

Having goals is one of the best and top-rated survival mindsets to have.

4. Eat anything that doesn't kill

You cannot go into the wilderness and begin to select the type of food to eat. You must be willing to eat whatever you find that does not kill so as to survive and keep on with your journey. Because you don't like eating insects does not mean you won't feast on them when the opportunity comes because staying alive is way better than being dead.

5. Have confidence

Be confident of yourself in bad situations that you will come out just fine. A survivor usually takes responsibility for several things and have to believe in themselves. Consistently, you must also be able to tell yourself that everything is fine.

There are several ways you can develop a survival mindset for a bushcraft situation. In the end, the type of survival mindset you have may be different from someone else's own.

Chapter 2

Bushcraft Survival Tips and Tricks

As a survivalist looking to go into the wild for one reason or the other, it is important to equip yourself with some useful tips and tricks to help you in your journey. The bushcraft survival tips and tricks are proven to offer a great deal of assistance in your wilderness experience. Check them out below:

1. **Know the fundamentals with the five Cs of surviving**

You need to equip yourself with the basic knowledge of the five Cs of surviving in the wild. For instance, the common five Cs of surviving includes:

- Choosing cordage
- Choosing a good shelter
- Choosing combustion tools
- Choosing the right tools
- Choosing a container

More will be discussed on this in chapter 3.

2. **Know how to plan and arrange your bag to take essential items**

It is not all about carrying a big backpack. You must take some essential materials and items like a first aid kit, tools, water bottle, tent, and so much more. All these will make your stay in the wild a bit stress-free.

3. **Test your kit on a short trip to ensure you don't overpack**

There is nothing worse than not being able to leave your backpack for a long time on your back. Bushcraft is mostly a long-term activity, so you need to watch your bag and drop any unnecessary things you won't need.

4. **Learn different knot types when setting up a tent**

- Are you looking to build a shelter? It would be best to learn the several types of knots, their uses and how to make one. This will go a long way in your journey as a survivalist. For the different knot types, I have you covered here https://www.amazon.com/dp/B08VLMR1VT

5. Know how to coil cordage so it won't tangle

This is a bushcraft skill needed, especially when building a short or long-term shelter in the wild. Usually, the cordage gets tangled, which is not an ideal situation to be in. However, before going to the wilderness, ensure you learn the process of adequately coiling the cordage.

6. Know different methods of striking a fire

Fire is significant as it serves different purposes in the bush, including calling for help, preserving food, and for vision. Learning the various methods of striking a fire is helpful in case one fails.

7. Learn how to differentiate good woods from bad ones

Woods are essential in a bushcraft survival situation. Differentiating the good ones from the bad ones is significant, especially when you want to ignite a fire or build a shelter.

8. Learn how to forage for food

You can barely stay for 48 hours without eating, and so food is a vital part of our daily life as human beings. To survive in the wild, you need to learn the different ways of foraging for food, especially in an awful situation where animals and insects are scarce.

9. Know how to disinfect water

If your water provision is finished, you will have to look for water and disinfect it before drinking. You wouldn't want to get dehydrated because it halts you from continuing with your journey.

Fortunately, water can be gotten easily, but the process of filtering and disinfecting it should be learned and followed before drinking to avoid illness.

10. Learn how to navigate

It is never a good situation when you are confused or lost about where to go and how to locate your built shelter. So, before going to the woods, ensure you have learned everything there is to know about navigating and moving from one place to another using compass and other means.

Being in a survival situation requires the mind and body to be functional at all times. However, your mind and body cannot be effective if you don't know how to go about certain things. Not to worry, because we have listed the different tips and tricks that will help you become a bushcraft expert.

Here is a quick one. Most of what is covered in this chapter will be discussed in detail as we proceed, so hold on tight.

Chapter 3

Gearing Up

The 5 C's of Survival

People usually go with several types of items in their backpacks, depending on the circumstance at hand. This is generally referred to as a survival situation, which is what endurance and survival represent. Over the past years, and through consistent practice, it is difficult to remove or add to some basic requirements. These things are reliant fundamentally on a particular assignment, ecological or occasional change, which is why the 5 C's of survivability cannot be overlooked. There are undisputable things that are absolutely necessary for any survival situation, including bushcraft survival.

The fundamentals of the 5 C's are the things that either need unique materials to build or take the most energy to make from natural materials in the woods in a survival situation.

Now, briefly consider being trapped in a 72-hour survival-type situation in the wild. What are the set of things you will do to survive or when low on provisions? A survival knife would be the major item for this kind of situation. With the right survival knife and a touch of understanding, you can make whatever else you need, such as holder, cordage, sanctuary, or fire set. These are basic things required in controlling your core temperature. CCT (Controlling Center Temperature) is the primary item needed in a survival situation because Hypothermia or Hyperthermia is the main reason for death or abandonment of people in the wild.

The five below-listed items can allow you to achieve your entire basic survival requirements, even if it is for a short time.

Choosing your survival knife and cutting tools

The cutting tool you are using ought to, at the very least, be able to complete your entire tasks if your other tools cannot keep up with the requirement. This is required from any tool you have selected.

A survival task tool ought to be something that isn't excessively huge as you may require it for fine cutting or food planning. You might have a little hand hatchet if you needed it for some essential tasks. Numerous individuals today appear to convey several tools or pocket knives for emergency purposes. They can be perfect as an additional tool because they can be helpful for other situations.

In any case, they ought to never be your first choice as they are not massive enough or sufficiently able to be the only tool you need in a survival situation. It's also suggested that your tool is produced using High Carbon steel and not pure or other extraordinary metal.

The knife span you chose as your survival tool must have a 90-degree level ground spine with the goal that it tends to be utilized for hitting a Ferro bar. This stops you from using the cutting edge and not waste its sharpness. The explanation behind the High Carbon steel sharp edge is for sparking flint or other hard materials.

Recall that the kit's items should have multiple purposes to dispose of the less needed weight and achieve more with lower options. The less weight idea is to save resources such as the calories used to convey your unit alongside the inadequate hydration from hefty loads.

Choosing your combustion equipment

Combustion equipment ought to be fit for the most value of money too. The main thing required from emergency combustion equipment is Surefire. It does not represent things such as lighters that could conceivably create an ensured fire in wet conditions.

With the combustion devices, it points to the direction of ferrocerium robs and mini infernos. They will function while wet or dry and deliver a definite fire for a few minutes to help in the start of marginal tinder sources such as damp shavings, barks, and semi-green vegetation. What should be acknowledged is that the mini inferno is an outright survival solution for making fire and ought to never be utilized if dry tinder is accessible nearby.

Choosing your shelter and cover equipment

Cover items can be little and strong but must carry out multiple tasks. It's ideal to convey a minimum of a poly tarp of 8x10, a six mil 55-lady garbage sack/drum liner alongside an emergency re-useable space cover.

This little roll will offer you huge loads of flexibility and versatility at a negligible expense. More uses for these things include the following:

- Sleeping bags
- Rain catchments
- Rain gear
- Signaling
- Ground coverings

Choosing a container

Containers are quite possibly the most significant parts of gear you will use at any point. Without having water, it may not be possible to survive for a long time, even after achieving CCT.

Hence, we should make sure the container can complete some tasks exceptionally well. It should be watertight, fit for being put into the fire for water sanitization and cooking. The container must be designed with thick-wall materials to hold the shock from being hit or dropped.

Choosing Cordage

Cordage is an unquestionable requirement to have, and it may be too tedious and challenging to make in a survival situation. There are two basic types of cordages and one is preferred over the other for a few reasons. Recently, the primary and most used cordage for any survival situation has remained the 550 parachute cord.

Genuine paracord contains seven inward strands with the goal that it very well may be separated for use on more little tasks like fishing. It is also excellent and light.

The main drawbacks to these inward strands are that they will always shred out, and they are hard to use for specific tasks such as trapping or catching the whole cord because it is enormous. On the other hand, the most liked and used cordage is something many refer to as Mariners Net Line or Tarred Bank Line.

They are not Masons line, which is sold at tool shops; this is unique. The Tarred Bank Line is three-handle cordage that is solid and can be bought up to 340 lbs breaking strength.

It occupies less space and weighs not exactly like paracord, although it is much more practical for things required in a survival situation like fishing, lashings, and trapping.

It is an extraordinary material for little game catches and traps and is additionally dark, which adds to its cover capacities when utilized for hunting and fishing. Furthermore, it extends lower than paracord, so bindings and lashings on shelters and tools don't extricate after some time.

Alongside its different uses, it is likewise sold around half as much as paracord and does not have enough weight. For what it is worth, it is viewed as a first cordage choice.

As we round up, understanding the five things and the complete uses for them is the initial step to knowing what it truly takes to lessen the size and weight of your kit and successfully keep up with surviving in the wild. What is much more imperative to comprehend is the expertise and capacity to supplement these things with natural material.

Bushcraft Camping Equipment

Regardless of whether you intend to stay in the wilderness for some days or weeks, the different bushcraft camping equipment will prove helpful for several reasons. The best thing to consider getting is less-costly bushcraft camping equipment that has good durability features.

This bushcraft camping equipment is useful, especially when situations call for it. As a matter of fact, you will use them, and so you need to get them ready and go with them whenever you are hitting the woods.

In this section, we have sub-divided the important bushcraft camping equipment into different groups, and they include:

Shelter and Sleeping Kit

Sleeping mat: Self-inflating mats offer more comfort than closed-cell foam mats. They also do not require too much space, and it is easy to carry along into the wilderness.
2. **Tarp:** The tarp is well-sized bushcraft equipment that forms a remarkable space beneath where to stay and not only sleep. Unlike a tent which offers

lesser space, the tarp provides more space. Waking up in a tarp will give you every bit of motivation to continue your journey in the wilderness. You can get different kinds of tarp models in stores.
3. **Sleeping bag:** Sleeping bags vary depending on the one that best fits the weather condition and the purpose of going into the wilderness. For weight-related purposes, goose-down bags are recommended, but for robust and easier-to-clean bags, synthetic bags are the go-to option.
4. **Bivvy bag:** There are several types of bivvy bags available on the market. Most of them are long-lasting, less-weight, not costly, and comfortable to wear. You can store things and more bushcraft tools whenever you are moving along the wilderness.

Carrying Kit

Carrying kits vary, and there are different types a survivalist can utilize while in the wilderness:

1. **Rucksack liner:** Although the rucksack liner is heavy, it is still able to tighten quickly and carry essential things you may need during your

bushcraft journey. An example is the Ortleib dry bag.
2. **Rucksack:** Examples of the rucksack carrying kit include Arkits side pockets and Karrimor SF sabre 45. They feature a draw-cord closure and clip-buckling fastening rather than zips which can cut on the slightest touch.

Cooking and Water

If you are looking to cook and filter water to drink during your bushcraft survival journey, then you should look through to know the equipment you need to get and store in your backpack.

1. **Spoon:** This is a kitchen utensil used for eating. The same use applies when you are in the wilderness.
2. **Water purifier:** A water purifier or filter is needed to make water safe and good enough to drink. Although boiling water through fire is a good option, but making a fire is not ideal in all situations. If that situation comes up, what then do you do? A water purifier will help you cleanse water even as you are moving in the woods.
3. **Billy can:** The billy can is a heavy bushcraft equipment that allows you to store water bags

and washbowl needed during your bushcraft survival journey. Whenever you need something, simply reach for your billy can and bring out the things you need.
4. **Water bottle and metal mug:** A clean water bottle and metal mug are required to store and drink water when you become dehydrated at a certain point in time.
5. **Another water bottle:** Perhaps, your first water bottle is finished, and you cannot stop at that moment to search and purify water; a second water bottle will save you all the stress. In all water bottles, you should fill-up a minimum of 3 liters.

Personal Hygiene

Personal hygiene is important to stay healthy and shun any form of illness. However, to remain healthy, you need also to embed personal hygiene into your bushcraft journey. Here are two kits needed to ensure this is done:

1. **Wash kit:** Carrying out personal hygiene outside your home is very crucial. A wash kit includes toothpaste, soap, toothbrush, razor and enough clean water. These are the important things in our

everyday life that we cannot do without, and they ensure our personal hygiene is still intact.
2. **Toilet kit:** When you are pressed, you will have to visit the toilet even in the wilderness. The toilet kit contains a small exped dry bag with wet wipes, cigarette lighter, alcohol hand-gel, and toilet paper. Instead of getting contaminated in the wilderness after releasing your waste products, you can easily use any toilet kits to remain safe and clean.

Clothing

Clothing is very vital in protecting likely animal predators from seeing and feasting on you. Furthermore, clothing is also essential because it protects us from harsh cold weather conditions.

Check below for the necessary clothing kits you should go with when going into the wilderness:

1. **Heavy warm layer:** These are wool shirts created in the woods. They won't be damaged even if they are brought close to the fire. In fact, warm heavy layers last for long periods.
2. **Extra clothes:** Since you are preparing for unexpected situations in the wilderness, it is

important to always go in with extra clothes. Extra clothes may include spare underwear, a shirt, pants, and socks.
3. **Bandana:** A large cotton bandana can be tied to your head to prevent the removal of your hair. Also, bandanas are vital because they can be used to filter water from microbes.
4. **Waterproof shell:** You can find a few amazing lightweight waterproofs in stores. They are mostly useful for climbing mountains and walking in the hills. For example, when there is a fire outbreak in the woods, a fire-proof jacket can best work to protect yourself from any potential harm.
5. **Sun hat:** A sun hat is essential to prevent the sun from hitting your head during sunny days. Heavy sun for long hours can make you feel exhausted and unwilling to push further in the woods. However, a sun hat will prevent the sun from directly impacting your eyes and face.
6. **Warm hat:** You can also get a lightweight and warm hat because it makes your head feel warm on some occasions.
7. **Lightweight warm layer:** A lightweight warm layer is usually worn in sleeping bags, especially if the weather condition is freezing. Do not wear

the lightweight warm layer as an outer layer because it will ruin them. Instead, wear them inside your main clothing layers. It contains a loop-stitching which you can pull.

Other important equipment or tools

Asides from the above-listed bushcraft survival equipment and tools, there are some other important ones that must also be considered as you journey into the woods:

1. First aid kits

In case of any bad circumstances such as injury, a first aid kit is needed to salvage the situation. This first aid kit can be stored in your bushcraft backpack and used anytime the situation demands it.

2. Head-torch

When everywhere becomes dark, a head-torch is essential for seeing. Without a reliable head-torch, you cannot strive or make moves in the night.

3. Binoculars

This is a bushcraft survival equipment that allows you to see your incoming threat or view the next step to take.

4. Blade

A blade is one of the top bushcraft survival tools which many survivalists should get. It can be used to slice or cut difficult things, depending on the survival situation at hand.

5. Firestarter

If you want to quickly make a fire for a specific purpose and don't want to stress yourself, a fire starter will better serve you. Examples of a fire starter include a Ferro rod or a flint.

6. Saw

This tool is perfect for cutting tree branches, cutting firewood, clearing grass or bushes among many others.

7. Cordage

This bushcraft survival tool is utilized to make shelter frames, build a fishing net, hang a bear bag, etc.

8. **Shovel**

A shovel is a vital bushcraft tool used to dig a hole, dig a latrine, or bury something like a waste product. Additionally, a shovel can also serve the function of building shelters and creating drainage systems.

9. **Knife sharpener**

Most knives and other cutting tools will most likely become dull after using them for long periods. When going on your bushcraft journey, you should also go with a knife sharpener if your cutting tool becomes blunt and you need to sharpen it.

10. **Compass**

It is crucial to learn and fully understand what it means to navigate with a compass. It would be challenging to locate a particular spot without one, and you may wander around for hours. The compass allows survivalists to find the nearest safe place to lay for some period until they figure things out.

11. **Footwear**

In addition to wearing clothes, footwear choice during your bushcraft journey is also important. You should be able to wear shoes or something that will cover your legs from getting hurt. Furthermore, endeavor to purchase durable footwear so it won't damage when walking in the woods.

12. Pot and cup

The pot is vital if you want to purify or cleanse water by boiling it under fire. On the other hand, the cup is used to take the boiled and cleansed water from the pot before drinking. Aside from boiling water to drink with the pot, it also serves to cook different kinds of food in the wilderness.

Everyone is allowed to choose their favorite, useful and needed bushcraft camping tool and equipment. The woods are not a very lovely place to be, especially if you are battling to survive. The bushcraft survival equipment and tools are of great importance, and no survivalist should think of leaving his house without the essential bushcraft survival tools.

A Short message from the Author:

Hey, I hope you are enjoying the book? I would love to hear your thoughts!

Many readers do not know how hard reviews are to come by and how much they help an author.

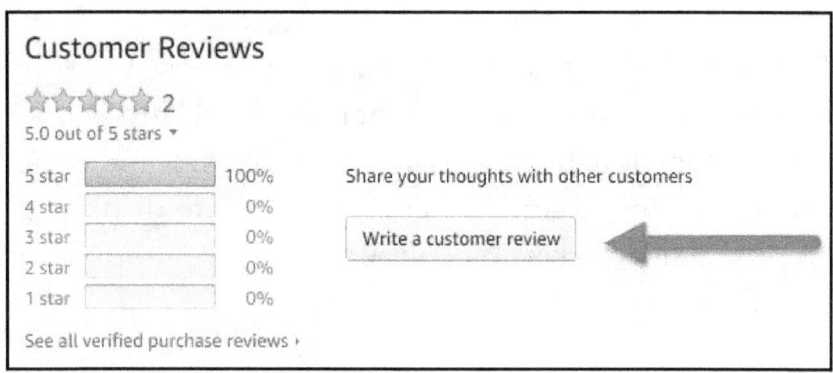

I would be incredibly grateful if you could take just 60 seconds to write a short review on Amazon, even if it is a few sentences!

\>> Click here to leave a quick review

Thanks for the time taken to share your thoughts!

Chapter 4

Surviving In The Bush

Building a Shelter for Warmth

A good shelter should be your first and significant survival priority because it protects you from predators and other dangerous animals. In fact, shelter is more important than water or food in a survival situation. That said, let's discuss ways you can build a survival shelter for warmth, as given below.

Find a Suitable Site

You should try to find a location that is perfect for building a shelter in the wilderness. The site must be dry, close to the sea, flat, not below any cliffs, and open. Contrary to these conditions above, your site won't be situated in the best place because anything can happen anytime.

Check Your Needs

Many wilderness survival professionals will inform you that this is the best way of surviving in the wild.

Meanwhile, it is dependent on your needs. Here are but a few questions you can ask yourself:

- Does your shelter need to take another form?
- What is the number of people in your group?
- Is the shelter for long or short use?
- How long will it take to build the shelter?
- What will be the weather condition of the shelter?

Some of the most important tools you should also check to include:

- Folding saw
- Bushcraft Axe
- Machete
- Survival knife

Know Your Type of Shelter

This is where you need to put all your effort and attention because it is the most crucial part of making a shelter in the wilderness.

There are several types of wilderness shelters you can erect. They include:

- **The Tarp Shelter**

This shelter only requires a plastic tarp and cordage. Additionally, you can build it using a rain poncho in a pinch. Simply tie the two ends of the tarp to a tree.

Advantages of a tarp shelter

1. Perfect for a large group of people
2. Quick to build
3. Easy and straightforward to build

Disadvantages

1. Lack of protection from animals and weather conditions

2. Can break easily from heavy rain

- **Tarp Tent**

For this shelter, you will have to wrap cordage between two trees and hang your tarp on it before using a few sticks, rocks to attach it to the sides

Advantages

1. Protects one from rain
2. Quick to erect

Disadvantages

1. It does not protect one from wild animals
2. Can break easily

- **Tarp Teepee using Poles**

Here, you have to arrange a few long poles and attach them to create the design for the teepee. Furthermore, tie your tarp around the branches.

Advantages

1. Best for large groups
2. Strong
3. Fire can be ignited inside it

Disadvantages

1. It might take some time to build
2. Requires large tarp
3. There will be an opening at the top of the tepee allowing for rain to enter

- **Tarp Teepee (Without poles)**

In this survival shelter, you need to fold your tarp into a triangle type of shape then place a rock inside the tarp. Proceed to wrap some cordage around the stone and hand the cordage from a tree. Attach the underside of the tarp using rocks.

Advantages

1. Protects from different elements
2. Offers extra shelter because of the tree

Disadvantages

1. It might be difficult to tie the cord to the tree branch
2. Requires a large tarp

- **Snow Shelter**

To create a snow shelter, get a tree, cut the branch at a 45-degree angle and pull the snow away to build a wall. Then cut another branch to help the tarp. Proceed to hand a tarp over the branches and line the inner part using pine needles.

Advantages

1. Can be created either small or large
2. Perfect for winter or cold survival circumstances

Disadvantages

1. Fire cannot be ignited inside it
2. Moving snow can waste time and dry out without using a shovel

- **Fallen Tree Shelter**

The fallen tree shelter can be built in different ways, like hanging a tarp on the fallen tree to create a tent. On the other hand, it can also be made by propping dirt to serve as the shelter wall.

Advantages

1. Easy to disguise
2. It can be built using dirt or a tarp
3. Adaptable to different situations
4. Perfect protection from snow and other elements

Disadvantages

1. It might require extended time to arrange the dirt
2. Because of the rotting log, bugs will enter the shelter

- **Hammock Survival Shelter**

In few situations, your survival shelter needs to be away from the ground, like jungle situations where several creepy and dangerous animals are found. To build the hammock survival shelter, simply line it using your additional clothes to offer some insulation.

Advantages

1. It is away from the ground

Disadvantages

1. It does not really protect you from dangerous elements, including rain
2. More tarps and cordage is needed for this shelter

- **A-Frame Brush Shelter**

This is a perfect survival shelter for hunters or survivalists looking to stay for a short time. It is also an ideal shelter for one person. The materials for building the A-Frame brush shelter are simple to get.

Advantages

1. For a single person
2. Easy to build
3. Can be a camouflage
4. Quick to build

Disadvantages

1. It is only for a short period
2. Fire won't warm in this shelter

Follow the steps below to build the A-Frame Brush Shelter:

1. Locate a long and strong branch. It should go some feet longer than your current height.
2. Prop an edge of a branch on a tree log. You can also prop it to create an A shape.
3. Lay short branches on the first branch to create a frame.
4. Close the frame using branches or leaves.

- **Debris Tipi Shelter**

The debris tipi shelter is easy to erect, but you will need to get long branches. The only drawback to the tipi shelter is that it is long and it is vertically shaped.

Advantages

1. Perfect for large groups
2. Simple to create

Disadvantages

1. It needs several long branches
2. Fire will not stay in the shelter
3. It is not advisable for high winds
4. Leafy branches should work to close the openings
5. It does not hold heat like other shelters

Follow the steps to build a Debris Tipi Shelter:

1. Locate three long branches that have similar lengths. Prop them to create a tripod frame. On the other hand, you can also prop the tree branches to create a special type of tipi shelter.

2. Include extra-long branches to the tripod you create. The frame will become strong if you include extra branches to it. Don't forget to leave an opening for the shelter's door.
3. Continue adding branches, even short ones.
4. Close the strong frame using leafy branches. Don't use a brush because it won't cover the structure.

- **Debris Lean-To**

The lean-to shelter is easy to build, and there is often enough room. It also does not hold the body heat, but the shelter's wall can serve as a fire reflector.

If you ignite a fire in the shelter's front, the heat will come off the wall and come at you. You can also make a fire reflector on the other part of the fire pit.

Advantages

1. It is simple and quick to build
2. Adding wind and bed screen to the shelter can serve you for a very long time

Disadvantages

1. It does not warm itself, meaning you need to ignite a fire.
2. It is not so camouflaged
3. Wind can enter from the sides

- **Brush Shelter using Smoke Hole**

There are several ways to create shelters with smoke holes. You can build a tipi kind of shelter and leave an opening at the top.

Advantages

1. Perfect for winter survival situations
2. It includes several likely designs

Disadvantages

1. It takes a long time to learn
2. It also requires a longer time to create because the smoke hole reduces its stable nature.

Navigating and Traveling In The Wilderness

Getting Lost and Found

Utilizing situational awareness skills and standard route strategies is the best protection against getting lost in the wild. Additionally, create a note of the time it requires to walk in a single direction.

To reduce the likelihood of getting lost on a trip to your camp, set up your base close to a river. Furthermore, move out in a genuinely opposite way from it.

When you are back, you will realize you need to turn either left or right when you arrive at the benchmark. Also, to be sure what direction you need to turn, you can deliberately move to one side of the camp while still waking. This requires near accurate prediction.

If you figure you may be lost, quickly pause and set up another beginning stage or base. Indent a tree, accumulate a few rocks, or bind a shiny material to a branch. When you are refreshed and thinking plainly, begin walking once more.

Follow steadily augmenting circles around the base as you look for natural landscape or the path you were on. As you go far away from the beginning point, twist branches or blast trees along your way so you can remain in line and know the route back.

Furthermore, mark your blazes so they can be seen as one or the other. Cut them into the bark corner to corner, with the blaze's higher-finish pointed toward the base.

One strategy for remaining on the same route as you move along is to arrange two trees or different tourist spots ahead as you walk. Suppose you begin seeing both of them one by one, pause and realign your stand with them. When you arrive at the subsequent tree, go through the same process by arranging two additional tourist spots that lie straightforwardly ahead.

Utilizing the Sun to Tell Time and Direction

Because the sun displays the vast majority of the day in the sky's southern area, shades are predominant in northern openings; this basic general rule can, in some cases, compensate for the absence of compass. Likewise, moss grows thickest on the rocks and trees' obscure side, so even on a shady day, you can know your cardinal focuses.

Stick and shadow technique: Because the sun heads out from east to west, shadows travel from west to east. Consequently, if you plant a stick in the ground, mark the finish of its shade with a rock and come back in about 20 minutes to mark the new spot where the shadow halted and place a stick between the two points. This will serve as your East to West direction, while the West is on the edge marked by the initial rock.

Utilize a watch to know South: Grip the watch at 12 o'clock to the left-hand side. Then change the direction of your arm, so the hour hand focuses on the sun. The spot somewhere between the hour hand and 12 o'clock becomes your south.

Added Direction Tips

Improvised compass: Press a needle or metal wire firmly on your head to magnetize it and further drop it in leaf water. If you stroke the needle from the eye downwards, the eye will move to the north.

Celestial Navigation: Around evening time, all stars circle Polaris, the north star, which does not change directions. The two stars on the external piece of the Huge Dipper's scoop move in the Polaris direction. The hunter moves SE to SW every night during winter. Also, your latitude on earth is equivalent to the point of your area focusing at Polaris.

Set up the denomination/map versus compass North: When figuring your direction with compass and mass, remember that the Earth's attractive poles are situated at unexpected areas compared to the topographical poles. In this way, a north-pointing compass will consistently push you to a direction that is a little off track from the topographical north on a guide. For example, in California, the compass north is 14 degrees east of guide north, while on the east coast, compass north is 10-25 west of guide north.

Evaluate the remaining sunlight: To decide how long it will be before sunset, lift the shut fingers of one hand between the sun and the skyline. Each finger carries 15 minutes and each hand 60 minutes.

Setting the right time on your watch: Utilize a pine needle to stamp a razor-meager shadow on the dial. Locate the midpoint between that particular line and 12 o'clock with the shorter arc. Then, turn the hour hand to this point.

Methods of Navigating and Traveling In The Wilderness

There are several methods to adopt when navigating or traveling in the wilderness. They include:

Instructions to Use the Watch Technique and Sundial:

For this method to work, you need the sun. If you point the hour hand of an analog watch at the sun, the middle way from the hour hand to 12noon on the watch dial will equal the South. Using a digital watch, you can assess the Watch dial with your hands or even copy an analog watch dial and store it in your survival backpack.

In terms of the shadow stick sundial, position a straight stick on a level smooth ground and mark the shadow's finish. Using a little stick, wait for 15 minutes or more and mark the new shadow. Proceed to sketch a west to an east line from the initial one to the subsequent shadow because the sun moves from East to west.

White Pine Trees

White Pine trees are sketched, designed and formed to point east; by the transcendent most solid northwest high pressing factor winds. They are often called the compass tree.

Magnetic Compass Bearings

There are five stages to a compass bearing. The essential method is to take a direction to dial your heading, like 0 to 360 degrees. For instance, dial East or 90 degrees, take the red magnetic needle into the orienteering arrow into the bezel and move towards the same direction as the arrow.

The further developed strategy includes:

1. Pick A to B direction on a topo map that seems to be okay.
2. Draw the compass baseplate's edge with the A to B line, ensuring that the bearing of movement direction is pointing from A (beginning stage) to B (finishing point).
3. Turn the housing so that the north orienteering arrow is focusing on the tipper map.
4. Fix your map bearing for the declination, like for the Frontenac District. Include 13 degrees because it is a westerly declination.
5. Take the red needle into the north orienteering arrow, and see your bearing through the movement arrow heading.

Geographical Maps:

Scales have different sizes. Pilots use 1:500,000 scale maps and welcome highlights, for example, air terminals, runways, seas, and mountains.

Outdoor tourists utilize 1:50,000 scale topos, like Soft map and Fugawi brand virtual products, and for more detail, while a few fishers use standard base guides, 1:10,000 scale.

The different maps are diverse depending on crown land maps and road maps that show you where topographical maps, nautical charts, and crown lands reside. Topos reveal to you the entire things on the top of the water, while nautical charts show everything underneath the water.

Map characteristics are seen in the legend, and significant ones incorporate a green image for swamps, green is forested, white is open country, intermittent lines are trails or logging streets, blu is water, dark dabs are homes, etc. Other helpful data include magnetic declination, map datum, and meter grid squares.

Hand-held GPS Units:

For land use, it would be best to get the Garmin-62 or 64s handheld models. If you like touchscreen with excellent graphics, the Oregon or Garmin Montana models are the best.

Denoting a Waypoint is straightforward. Simply switch on the unit, hold on to be in acceptable satellite inclusion, like under ten meters precision, and hit the market or save button. Continuously give the waypoints a name, else you won't recollect a number.

Moving to discover a waypoint is simple, just hit the find or go-to option, look over your saved focuses, and pick one.

Breadcrumb Trails can also be enabled in set up and menu.

Important tip: Endeavor to always go with a physical map and compass alongside your GPS unit. The reason is that they do not require batteries to work, and they can be relied on.

Finding, Cooking, and Preserving Food

When you find yourself in a survival scenario, ensure you begin your food search whenever you are still healthy and agile. Most individuals make the mistake of searching for food when they are already tired; hence, their inability to find the best food to consume.

It is not easy to go hungry, and you won't even move further to survive in the woods. While finding food, you should make sure you stay away from lean meat like rabbit meat. This is because it is likely to result in diarrhea. Most food seen in the woods contains fat, and it is not advisable to be consumed.

Finding Food

Slow-Moving Animals, Lizards, Snakes, Frogs, etc

Cut a spear from a branch, utilize stones or sticks to catch your prey: Check what you can do:

Porcupines: These creatures have greasy meat that can sustain you. You can kill them quickly with a hit to the head. Keep away from contact with the plumes. Assuming you have a canine or other pet, keep it restricted and away from the porcupine. To eliminate the plumes, skin the creature beginning from the underside. Lighting plumes in a fire before cooking is not advisable.

Scorpions and Snakes: Remove the heads of venomous snakes and the stingers of scorpions. Discard these cautiously (for example, cover them profound and far from pets). Scorpions can be eaten raw or cooked. As a rule, the tiny ones have dangerous toxic substances and not the bigger ones. For snakes, skin and eliminate the guts before cooking. Remember that their bladders can be utilized to hold fluids.

Turtles: This is another source of greasy or fatty meat. Be cautious about turtle jaws and paws, even after killing the animal. At that point, heat the entire animal to make the back shell soft. Take it out before the undershell. Remove the cover before consuming the meat.

Game Creatures

It's not in every case legitimate or straightforward to discover and kill deer and moose, so look at the many game creatures accessible when attempting to stay alive in the wild.

Remember that creatures that have been pestered or pursued before the slaughter discharge lactic corrosive into their muscles. As a result, it makes the meat more short-lived, so plan to eat it the very day. On the other hand, give the creature time to recuperate by catching it whenever it allows and eliminate it later.

To make a catch, balance a massive circle of rope or twine across the way a creature will probably cross. You can lead the animal toward that path by setting up impediments or potential branches that seem to facilitate the passage along the way. Like individuals, animals usually take the least demanding route accessible.

Most game-winged creatures can be sought after because they don't fly a far distance.

Rabbits: These are a perfect source of lean meat, so consume them cautiously or join with fattier food sources. Rabbits regularly depend on the cover instead of departure from their hunters, so act like you didn't see one as you move towards it.

Beaver, bear and lamb: They are perfect sources of greasy meat.

Quail: Simple to find since they don't go far. You can set up a channel and cage them in so they can only escape with high effort.

Eggs: You realize you're close to a nest when a bird bombs you as you pass by the area. While recovering, attempt to leave a portion of the eggs to protect the up and coming age of accessible prey.

Fish and Other Seafood

Although they give adjusted nourishment, trout and numerous kinds of panfish do not give too many calories. A fat salmon, notwithstanding, can offer a significant number of calories (900) in food.

Improvised Hook: Cut or hone the edge of the two sides of a two-inch pencil-sized stick and conceal it in a trap. When a fish swallows it, pull the line, which turns the stick opposite and stays in the fish's throat.

No-Hook Fishing: There are a few different methods to get fish other than the hook and line method:

- Create a basket by adjusting a green branch into a casing, and join a cross-section of leaves or permeable fabric around the frame.
- Pursue fish from a stream into a pool with no way out and cover the entrance with wood or rocks.
- Around evening time, use light and lance to catch fish that meander into pools or swirls, attracted by the light. Point towards his back, where he is not able to see. Or then again pin the fish to the base, and get him with your hand.

- Bind a fabric to a line as a trap, and when the fish nibbles, quickly toss him on the shore.

To plan and organize fish for cooking, cut it with your blade on the belly part, from the butt-centric vent to the head. Proceed to take out the guts. Then grab it by the tail and remove the scales, veins and kidneys. For dish fish, leave the head, fins, and tail joined, so the bones remain as they are. Consume around the other parts.

To safeguard fish for future use, slice the flesh into small strips and leave to dry. For long haul stockpiling, dry out the filets by warming them enveloped by green leaves and set on a mesh on a low fire.

Seaweed: Different kinds of seaweeds are consumable and high in nutrients and minerals, with green growth giving one of the world's most protein-rich nourishments. Seaweed can be consumed raw or cooked in soups. You can likewise dry out and store them. Numerous youngsters prefer the dried form of seaweed.

Crabs: All are eatable, yet like other shell-fish, you shouldn't kill them until cooking time to evade potential poisons delivered in their body. Salt-water assortments (for example, trapped in the sea) can be consumed raw or cooked; land crabs might have parasites in them, so these should be cooked.

Sea cucumbers: The cucumbers develop close to the shore. Locals dry and smoke the five white long muscles. Scratch off the skin and discard the other parts.

Abalone: This is a vast stone sticking mollusk. Meddle it off the rock by slipping a long blade beneath it and snapping it uphill. Be mindful not to touch the shell because it can serve as a bowl later on.

Clams: Besides the Pacific shore underneath the Aleutian Islands, the dark meat of salt-water assortments should not be consumed between April and October. Around these months, clams eat harmful ocean living beings that cannot be eradicated by heat. The white meat is not wrong to cook consistently.

Sea urchins: Urchins contain eggs that can be consumed either raw or cooked. But do not consume starfish.

Mussels: These ought to be verified to ensure the shell closes firmly whenever it contracts. If it doesn't close firmly, keep away from it. Pale blue dark mussels joined to shell rocks should not be consumed between April to October because they also have the same issue as the clams mentioned above.

Other Sources of Nutrition

Animal Blood

Blood gives total nutrition and fluid without a water source. Blood is likewise plentiful in nutrients, iron and added minerals. About 4 tsps can be just about as nutritious as ten eggs. Furthermore, it does not taste as terrible as you might suspect. When butchering creatures, in a survival situation, consistently channel the blood into a type of holder or can.

To cook the blood, make a stock with it. Include wild vegetables if you are with one.

Skin and Bones

Animal skin can offer the same vitamins as lean meat. Contingent upon the circumstance, rawhide might be better used as shoemaking material.

Bones have numerous minerals and can be rescued whenever found with a creature's cadaver eliminated by another animal. Remove the marrow from giant bones and proceed to cook. The less cooked, the more vitamins it will have. Lesser bones can be utilized for soup.

Vitamin C

Commonly ignored in most bushcraft survival situations, Nutrient C is fundamental for wellbeing, and an absence of it brings about scurvy. Cooked food may not contain Vitamin C if it is over-cooked and contains too much salt.

Consume the starchy green tips of spruce needles raw to get a substantial portion of Vitamin C. Drink spruce or pine needle tea as a glass of squeezed orange to receive the Vitamin C measure almost multiple times.

Insects

When you are without an option, insects give a phenomenal nourishment source in little amounts. The main part of a survival diet is fat, and bugs are 100% fat. You can get them utilizing a light or light fire around evening time. While the day is still bright, turn over a dead log or exhume them from a live tree.

Remove termites from tree openings with a stick but be cautious because they can bit. You can typically spot hatchlings inside trees because the wood is already puffy.

Except for hard segments, wings, and any parts of harmful discharges, all body parts of bugs are generally eatable. Eliminate a grasshopper's legs, wings and head before consuming raw or cooked.

Spiders, ants and moths are consumable. For red ants, lift them by the head and remove their backside before eating. The other type of ants that usually bite will contain formic acid that can bother your stomach, so make sure you warm them or, better still, cook them first whenever the situation allows.

Cooking Food

Continuously make sure to clean your hands thoroughly after dealing with the game or stock creatures. Always endeavor to cook all meat to prevent illness, parasites, or germs.

A forked green stick fills in like a stick for simmering fish or meat. Push the substance momentarily in the fire to cover juices before cooking it elsewhere. You can then fold the meat over a stick to cook it, or divide the stick and supplement the meat in the middle before tying each end firmly. Place the divided stick between two crotched uprights over the fire.

For fresh meat, cook just as long as needed to procure the most nourishment. If accessible, you can utilize clusters of greenery as stove gloves.

Make a grill: Design a piece from green hardwood. Additionally, you can fix the fish to it and put that above the coals. Eliminate the animal's spine if the skin does not lay level enough. Proceed to turn the fish or meat about two times. Birch consumes effectively yet gives a decent smell. A level stone can likewise function as a slab; however, do not use stones that have been in the water.

Fast and filthy oven: For food that needs a few hours to cook, hot stones provide long-lasting descent heat. Make them heated up in a fire from the start and allow them to remain hot by drenching them with boiling water. Concerning the oven, dig an opening, line it with hot, dry stones, and place it on green leaves. This allows you to cover the entrance to enclose the heat. Permit a few methods for pouring bubbling water onto stones so that they can heat once more. Then again, you can light a fire in a little opening to warm the part.

Soup Opening: Line a hole opening with animal hide. You can add water, food and hot stones. Furthermore, you can pull out the cool rocks sooner or later and throw in recently heated rocks to keep the soup hot.

Clay cooking: You can assemble a straightforward clay oven utilizing a green-stick confine as its edge. Allow each layer of clay to dry first. To facilitate this procedure, make light flames inside the cage. When prepared for cooking food, pre-heat the stove by making a fire inside it and removing the ashes and adding foot on the leaves or stones.

Barbeque: Allow survival fire to consume the hot coals and lay green sticks over them. Juices prefer to stay if you do not cut the meat.

Tripod: Place a few branches with forked tops against one another teepee-style and make them comfortable so they will hold a heap. Then, tie shoelaces to the top to hang a pot above the fire.

Hot water without a holder: Here, you can light a fire in a stone cavity to preheat it. On the other hand, make fire around the stone pit. You can also utilize a compartment created out of wrapped birch bark and throw a hot stone into the water.

Dressing Animals: This technique is somewhat unique with all species; however, all in all, you need to:

- Eliminate the digestion tracts quickly because any substance inside may affect the meat.
- Keep the game warm. Before cooking, a temperature over 40 °F is not advisable for the meat.

Birds: Eliminate the quills when it is warm. Take out the pouch beneath the neck, and slice or tear open body with your hands above and underneath the ribs. Eliminate the stomach organs but do not touch the liver and heart. Clean the gizzard, and it will be acceptable to consume.

Deer Game: Punch a little hole directly underneath the bosom bone. Gases will get away and presumably will not have the best smell. After the gases go out, make an entry point right down to the pelvis. You also have to open up the hole and remove the digestive organs from the animal's stomach. Cut the trachea and remove all the connections of the heart and pull out the chest content. Proceed to separate the liver and heart.

Turn the creature aside and allow the whole blood to come out. The entirety of the internal parts should be removed. If not, slice the areas that are as yet connected to the inner portions. The digestion tracts will, in any case, be connected to the body by the rectal cylinder. This cylinder must be totally and neatly taken out. Surround the rectal cylinder a couple of times until it is removed.

You may need to slice from the inner part and remove it. Be cautious about the bladder and the stool tube. Getting both of these two waste materials on the meat can make the meat sharp. Pull the cylinder through the opening and completely drain the animal by moving aside. The vent opening will fill in as a channel when you hang the animal.

Little Game: It could be simpler to initially hang an animal in the air by holding its rear legs. Secure the depleted blood for soup, as it's profoundly good for the body. Slice the animal around every lower leg.

Cut within its legs to attach an extended cut between the vent and throat. From there, you can pull down and eliminate the hide. Open the animal from the vent to the ribs and eliminate its innards. Secure its kidneys, liver, and heart, which can be consumed. Assuming it is a muskrat animal type, remove its white tacky aroma organs from inside its thighs and forelegs.

Jerky: When consuming jerky, recall that it is lean and should be followed by fatty food sources to prevent diarrhea. Extensively cook fat pieces in oil and blend the oil in equivalent parts with jerky to make a sausage. Then keep the Pemmican in a watertight holder. It gives total nourishment but no Vitamin C.

Preserving Food

While in the wild, you will surely need something to eat. Meanwhile, if you came into the woods prepared, then finding food won't be an issue.

After capturing a deer or any other animal, killing it and consuming its meat, but with some leftovers, what do you do?

You cannot just leave it and allow it to waste because you may need it later when hunger comes calling once more. The best thing to do is to preserve the meat.

Ways to Preserve Meat

There are three things you need to do to preserve your meat. They include:

1. Keeping it cool.
2. Keeping it dry.
3. Keeping it clean.

Keeping Your Meat Cool

You can preserve your meat by keeping it cool. Simply remove the meat from the animal's bone and take out all linking tissue and fat.

Once all this is done, it will take away insulation, making it cool way quicker. Furthermore, the wind from outside can also help in preserving your meat by making it cool.

Keeping Your Meat clean

Ensure your meat is free from dirt. Utilize wipe water to remove any dirt or blood.

Keeping Your Meat Dry

This is an essential aspect of preserving your meat. This is where you need to analyze various strategies and sort out which one is best for you.

The most important method of drying your meat is to utilize sunlight. Cut the bits of meat into dainty strips. This is significant, as thicker parts will take more time to dry out. After cleaning, cooling, and drying the outside of the game, position it high in a tree. Ensure that the bits of meat hang in direct sunlight. The sunlight and heat will dry the meat and remove any germs.

You can likewise dry the meat with smoke or salt. Placing salt on meat is a fast method of drying meat, unlike smoking that requires many wood planks and takes a lot of time.

Preserving Meat Using Salt

The inclusion of salt in meat is likewise called curing or corning. There is no doubt that corned beef doesn't imply that the cows consumed several corns; it means that the meat was cured with salt grains.

There are two fundamental techniques for curing meat, a dry and wet cure.

Wet curing

Wet curing includes making a saline arrangement, around 14-20% salt in the water. Sugar can be included for flavor and to assist in fighting microscopic organisms.

Cut the meat into pieces and dunk it into saltwater for around five minutes; at that, hang the parts under sunlight.

As a result, the water will go up, and you will find a microcrystalline opposition of salt. It dries the meet quicker than direct sun and gives an unfriendly environment for any microbes that reside around it.

Dry curing

To use dry curing, get a lot of salt and add sugar and different flavors. This will serve as your dry rub.

Interestingly press against the rub on the bits of meat, ensuring they are all around closed, and keep them in your container, ideally impenetrable. Assuming you layer them, guarantee sufficient salt between the layers that no two bits of meat come against one another.

Preserving Meat Using Smoke

Another great strategy to preserve meat is to smoke the meat.

Smoking dries out the meat, alters the surface to be acidic, making it hostile to microscopic organisms, and incredibly tasty.

An important note to consider is that smoking is not cooking. You wash the meat in the smoke created by the fire; however, don't let a lot of heat from the fire enter the meat.

Your choice of wood is also significant for the last meat flavor. It would be best if you considered getting a hardwood with a decent aroma.

The likes of hickory, oak, cherry, maple, and applewood are popular woods you can utilize.

Stay away from sticky woods like pine because you wouldn't want it to enter into your meat. This implies staying away from newly cut wood, as that green wood will be excessively brimming with dampness and will create wet smoke.

Make sure you utilize dry wood. Dry and spoiled wood, otherwise known as punky wood, is almost excellent; it smokes well.

If you reside in a particular location for a long time, you should build a smokehouse. It is a square building that has eight-foot, and it is made of a square.

Smoked meat will last more and has a deep flavor.

How Long Does Wild Preserved Meat Last?

After preserving your meat in the woods, it's important to know how long this preserved meat can stay without spoiling.

- Daylight and citrus extract will preserve your meat for a few days. The citrus acid has the

advantage of having the option to be applied once more.
- Curing and smoking can preserve your meat for an extended period that may span up to a month.
- Making jerky may be the best long-haul technique because it lasts as long as a quarter of a year (3 months). However, it may be the most untasty and generally irritating to consume over a long period.

Finding, Filtering, and Disinfecting Water

Most bushcraft and wilderness survival professionals suggest that you can only stay three days without water in the wilderness. However, it does not represent the fact that you must find a water lake or fountain. Water can be found all around the wilderness except in the desert. Asides from finding water, this section will also discuss how to filter and disinfect the water for safe consumption.

Finding Water

There are some standard rules to follow before you begin to look for water. The first of them is that water mostly flows downhill. Rain and snowmelt pile up on the ground and create creeks, basins, and streams. The increase of green remains even when the water dries up; this clearly shows that it is stored under the earth's surface. There is every chance that water can be seen just a foot under the surface in a rock riverbed. Asides from creeks and streams, you can search for water on the north side of trees and hills. You can check for water below the hill, below a rock outcrop, below a ravine, and in a narrow canyon. Additionally, large rocks with crevices and cracks can keep or hoard water.

Capillary action is the only exemption to the downhill rule where water can be found. You may regularly locate large amounts of water in a few trees in the spring. More instances of capillary action are spring. Watch out for a healthy and large tree in dry terrain, and you may find some amount of water there.

Across the world, large amounts of water are kept in aquifers. This situation needs you to search or dig a well because moisture may be stored underneath the ground. Also, if you are hitting the road where people previously reside, chances may be that you will find previously built wells you can collect water from.

Whenever you are looking through a dry riverbed, you may feel water underneath by just walking on the bed without footwear. In fact, you may be fortunate to dig on the inner part, and you will find a place filled with water.

More ways to locate water is by finding heavily trafficked game trails downhill. Simply search for tracks and a lot of droppings. During your search, you will most likely come across a water hole.

Seawater

Even though seawater is not so healthy and can harm your kidneys, a few stories have suggested that taking small quantities over a period cannot harm you. Meanwhile, it is much more advisable to mix or combine it with fresh water if available.

Scan the upper part of the sea, which has lower salt and take them. Water generated from icebergs does not affect the human body negatively. You can drink ice from the iceberg that has sufficient sunlight. Additionally, blue ice has less salt, which makes it ideal for drinking.

Assuming you are with any plastic on your boat, it can serve as the condensation procedure to make water from the vapors that reside above the sea. Simply remove the condensed water from tarps and sails. If you go through an inland water source, chances are that the water around there is already diluted to drink. Taking a small quantity of salt is not bad, especially if you stay under the hot sun for a couple of days. Meanwhile, consuming saltwater directly can be toxic to your kidneys and make you sick.

Additional methods of finding and taking raw water include:

- Take advantage of the morning dew before it goes up by tying a cotton shirt on your lower leg and passing through the high grass. Whenever the shirt becomes saturated, go on to take out the water inside a bowl or cup.

- Search for tangles of alter, palm trees or reeds, cottonwoods or willow, because they also grow close to the waterways.

- Most individuals also use water witching for millennia to search for underground water sources. You can utilize a forked willow branch of steel with a single end directed at 90 degrees to create a handle. When it comes to the branch, sloppily hold the other fork end and move. Assuming the willow notices any water, it would move towards the water. In terms of the steel rods, sloppily hold the bent sides in two hands, while two straight ends will be on your hands parallel to each other and the ground. Assuming water is under the surface, the two ends will bend like a magnetic force attracts it.

- A few vehicle radiators have water, and you can take it by loosening the lower bolt using pliers. Afterward, position a pan below to get the outflow. However, do not forget to filter and boil the water before taking it. Don't also drink anti-freeze because the chemical solution present is very harmful.

In rare circumstances where you cannot find water of any kind, you can use the liquid moisture in animals, fruits, plants, and fish to remain hydrated. Look below for a few instances:

- A few cacti have water. However, endeavor to cut off the spines before drinking the resulting liquid moisture.

- People usually drink edible palm fruits, prickly pear, and berries to derive water. But make sure you spit out the remains once you have taken the moisture.

- Get the moisture from a fig tree. Ensure you bring along a tube and container to retrieve the moisture after drilling a hole into the fig tree.

- Green coconuts have water that can be taken. On the other hand, brown coconuts have milk. However, you are expected to drink it carefully to prevent diarrhea.

- Open plant stalks, thick vines, and bamboo with your hands to search for moisture. Meanwhile, do not ingest the liquid directly from the roots because it can be harmful.

- Dead camels, fish, and other safe animals have water in them. However, you should get a bowl to retrieve the water while cutting them open.

- Turtle and bird blood can also offer moisture.

- If you are convinced rain is about to fall, simply place large leaves, bamboo cut, or seashells sliced into half to retrieve and retain the lost water.

More Places To Find Water

Check out a few more places where water can be found:

- **Underground springs:** This is mostly seen close to volcanoes and forests. Search for wet grounds and water emerging from cracked rocks.

- **Swamp water:** Look through the water on the top and remove the debris.

- **Change snow:** Here, you will have to dig up the existing snowfall to locate water. The powder contains a small amount of water, while ice contains a high amount of water. To melt it, pour a small amount in the pot and heat it but do not overheat it. Continue adding snow while it is melting inside the pot. Surprisingly, frozen water can still contain germs, which means you need to filter it before drinking.

- **Wells:** Under every land, you will find a water table. This is usually situated under the ground, but wells have been dug for ages now. If you can see an old one, it will still contain water that can be consumed, especially when filtered.

Making Water Via Condensation

This section's major piece of information uses a joint effort of heat and glass to change contaminated water into clean water. You can take liquid from green leaves and seawater because salt may not change to vapor. Sun is the primary heat source. However, a small amount of fire can also serve as a heat source.

Check out some methods of making water through condensation:

- **Solar distiller:** A solar distiller is usually a box containing a center and an open top. One part of the box has more height than the other part. In fact, you can utilize clear plastic or plexiglass to close it. Ensure it is positioned to bend down, allowing the condensed drops created on the inner part to fall outside. The remains will move to the clean water area and emerge from the box into a clean and different container.

- **Solar still:** In this instance, you have to dig a 3 by 3-foot hole in a location where it seems like water may have been taken beneath the ground previously. Proceed to line it using a sheet of 6 by 6-foot clear plastic, alongside a rock in the plastic center to form a shape similar to a cone.

Below the plastic, you can use a similar container size of a big coffee cup. As the process goes on, the container will secure the falling condensation into the plastic from every side. To retain and keep the plastic sheet in position, endeavor to close its edge with rocks. While below the hold, you can position a grass or cacti that will also add to the condensation.

- **Fire in metal containers:** Attach a lantern underneath a large container, ignite it, and close the container, but do not try it in an air hole. Furthermore, place the container in the toxic liquid. Afterward, condensation will convert the drinkable water into the container when it is heated.

- **Transpiration:** Locate a sunny area and cover a plastic bag with a large leaf branch. Ensure the plant is not toxic. Oak or willow is useful for this process. Also, ornamentals are not suitable, as well as leaves that bring out white substances when open. Instead, search for leaves that are small and have a little green. Then tie the open part of the bag to the branch. Be cautious and watch out for sharp objects that can cut small holes in your bag.

Filtering Methods

Anywhere you find water, you are not expected to drink it until you have filtered it. However, if the circumstance at hand is terrible, you should go ahead to drink it and purify yourself later.

Virtually everywhere you find yourself in, you will find contaminated water because some animals defecate and urinate in the water. Additionally, dead bodies may even enter the river, which can lead to toxic situations. Coldwater is safe to drink without treating it because the microbes are more effective in warm surroundings. Meanwhile, microbes are not the only things you should bother yourself about. Rigid metals like arsenic, mercury, lead, and copper seen in streams and coming down from mountains are very toxic to the human body.

Water gotten from rainwater contains a high-altitude underground spring, meaning it might not need to be filtered. The essence of filtering is to cleanse the water from the organic metal metals, gravel and slit, which may have piled up.

To filter water, you are advised to utilize a plastic container, a seashell, a bowl shape, or a soak. Furthermore, you can also get a funnel out of organic materials such as grass and bark. The most recommended mode of filter should contain multiple layers that your liquid will pass through, beginning from the coarsest material.

- **Charcoal**

Charcoal gotten from the campfire is one of the best ways to filter out harmful chemicals. This substance contains several crooks and crannies inside it, making it possible to hold unwanted microbes. Bag carriers usually contain filters that have activated carbon.

These substances are retrieved from a carbonaceous material made to create an added porous. On the other hand, it is not difficult to make your charcoal using a burning nutshell, peat, coal, or wood fire.

However, always recall not to use the same charcoal repeatedly because the holes will fill up and permit pathogens to pass through.

- Red sphagnum moss present in marshes and bogs is another good enough filter because it has natural iodine to disinfect and filter water simultaneously. If you are fast about something, you can simply squeeze water from the moss and pour it into your mouth. However, it is much more advisable to take the moss and pour the water into it while filtering it using a cloth before drinking it.

Some other filtering recommendations:

- Pour toxic water through thick-woven cotton or sock to differentiate the live organisms from the clean water.

- Get a funnel out of a shape that looks like an ice-cream strip of birch bark. Other layers of gravel, charcoal, sand, and grass can also work fine. Also, utilize a scarf on the catch container, and it will serve as the last filer.

- Assuming a spring or pond seems to be murky, dig into the gravel about two feet far away. Furthermore, the water in the hole from underneath is always naturally filtered by the sand and silt. Also, close the mouth of your container using a cloth and allow it to cover the water.

A piece of information to always remember is that filtering water will only reduce the number of microbes and not eliminate it. Also, harmful substances such as arsenic are still likely to enter. Assuming you reside close to an urban area, livestock is, agricultural or power plant spot, you should be very careful when filtering water.

On the other hand, when staying in the wilderness, getting toxins is way less. Furthermore, the higher the altitude, the higher the pristine the land receives. You can try getting cold water from the river because it is much more likely to be safe and less contaminated, unlike other water sources.

Disinfecting Water

Water gotten through evaporation, underground spring, rainwater, and condensation does not need to be disinfected. Meanwhile, if you are not convinced about the water's safety, you should not hesitate to disinfect it.

To disinfect your water, you can check out the different ways:

- **Boiling:** If there is fire around you, you can use it to disinfect your water. In fact, boiling water under fire is one of the fastest ways to kill microbes. Within 10 minutes, your boiled water should be free from virtually every microbe and safe to drink.

- **Bleach:** Liquid bleach works perfectly for disinfecting water and not the powder type of bleach. Simply pour a teaspoon of liquid bleach into the water, shake and wait for about 30 minutes before drinking it. Do not use powder or scented bleach because it can be harmful to the human body.

- **Distillation:** Utilizing a solar still can keep the microbes underneath the bowl or pot. However, a few heavy and contaminated metals may always be present. After distillation is done, shake the container to oxygenate the water. As a result, it will take away any likely flat taste.

- **Iodine:** With a 1 teaspoon of iodine tablet, you can easily disinfect your water in under 3 minutes. After using iodine to disinfect your water in a container, make sure you shake the container and allow the water to leak out to disinfect the drinking surface. Also, endeavor to wait for half an hour if the water is cold.

- **Solar/UV Ray:** If the above-listed methods are not accessible, simply give your water to the heat and light the sun offers. When the sun is hot, leave your water under it for 60 minutes, and it will disinfect. Meanwhile, if it is a cloudy day, you can leave the water open for some hours.

Professionals opined that UV rays only enter up to about 4 inches into clean water. However, if the water is dirty, the solar or UV ray method will not be effective. While using this method, make sure you use a plastic or bottle glass to hold the water because window glass won't work.

Effects of drinking contaminated water

As mentioned earlier, contaminated water is not good, and it can be harmful to the human body. The essence of filtering and disinfecting dirty and toxic water is to stay healthy. Toxic water has several disadvantages, and it comes with different types of sicknesses.

Here are but a few causes of drinking contaminated water:

- Cholera
- Typhoid

- Giardia lamblia
- Cryptosporidium

Making a Fire

Making a fire is key to surviving in a wilderness when hunting or carrying out some other task. Because cigarette lighters may not come up and matches are likely to get wet, you should endeavor to learn different methods of making a fire in the wilderness.

Regardless of the fire you want to start; you should consider the following things first:

- **Fuel:** Large branches, charcoal, or split logs or optional long-burning object or item can keep the fire on for a very long time.
- **Kindling:** Twigs or any small branches that ignite fire quickly should also be considered.
- **Tinder:** Straw, cotton, wood shavings, dry grass, pine resin, lichen and more flammable material that quickly ignite the fire for a long time must be considered.

You are expected to produce sparks of light to ignite the tinder. On the other hand, you can opt for mineral-rich rock or steel, battery leads, concentrated sunlight, steel wool, or electrical wiring to generate light.

Without any of the above-listed options, you may need to produce a spark with friction by pressing a wood stick on a wooden hole. Meanwhile, you have to perform this after generating the spark you need.

Below are some unique methods for making a fire:

- **Bow and drill method:** This is more like an old method of starting a fire. It is also a method of making a fire that requires work to be done. In this step, fire is generated when friction is made by running wood on a small pole consistently until the fire is ignited.

  Then again, a long vine or twine can work perfectly by pulling it back and forth on wood to ignite a fire. Although this procedure may require some time to do, you must heat the fire close to 800 degrees F for the fire to be kindled.

- **Yucca wood method:** This method of making a fire is usually seen in arid climates with low ignition. To make this possible, simply slice two strong 6-8 strips and tie them together using a pebble on every end to permit air to enter. Then create an extra 12-16 inch strip before rubbing it in the space to produce a fire.

- **Flint striker:** Many survivalists are always with a flint striker because they usually utilize it alongside a knife or any steel to create sparks. Meanwhile, if you are without any of these, quartz, iron pyrite, jasper, native jade, agate, and more mineral-rich rocks can produce increased heat when hit against each other.

  Furthermore, you can also create sparks by hitting the rock against your knife's rear side, especially if your knife is made of high-carbon.

- **Focusing sunlight method:** With a magnifying glass, binocular lens, aluminum, camera lens, broken glass, you can ignite a fire. Simply concentrate a light ray on your tinder to generate a fire after some minutes. This method is very effective if the weather condition is dry and hot. Also, ensure your tinder is very dry.

More fire tips

There are tons of different kinds of tinder accessible to survivalists in the wilderness. While hiking, try to watch for dry moss, grass, evergreen needles, pussy willow fuzz, lichen, nests, dry fungi, pith from elderberry shoots, dry-rot wood, bark fungus, dry veggie fibers, and goldenrod heads. More so, liquid resin is kept in the knots and blisters of pine trees, and it emerges whenever your cut inside of it. Furthermore, birch bark is also effective when you cut an extended part of it and roll it up for a long time.

Long fire: This is useful for cooking different dishes and offering warm conditions when sleeping under cold. Simply utilize the underside of the rock cliff to generate heat from the other side of the fire.

Additional kindling and fuel sources: Softwood such as scales and needles create the ideal kindling. Meanwhile, hardwoods like hickory, elm, oak, beach, chestnut, maples, tamarack, spruce, and white pine make a hot and extended fire.

No-wood fire: This method is a drop melted animal fat down on a rack of bones staying on the top of a little kindling fire.

Sleeping warm: Here, heat or fire up the ground meant for sleeping by merely burning fire on its surface. Also, make a fire on the two sides of your outdoor bedding and dig a trench to guard yourself against entering into the fire. You can also cover it with evergreen boughs and wrap them with rocks to stop the fire from getting to it. Heated or fired stones such as hot water bottles can work perfectly here.

Wood pile: If you want to make a log storage device close to a fire, you are expected to utilize two stakes, two diagonal poles moving from front to back, and two vertical support poles at the rear side.

Things That Bite, Maul, Sting, or Make You Sick

While in the wilderness, you are prone to experience or come across insects that can bite, maul, sting and even make you sick. The bites and stings from dangerous insects can result in severe health dangers.

If you are preparing to go into the wilderness, get ready because these insects will also be on the same journey as you. The likes of mosquitoes and other annoying insects are there to spoil the fun you may likely have when foraging foods or disinfecting water to drink, among others.

Because of this, it is crucial to plan and prepare yourself for your outdoor experience in the woods so as not to fall sick and possibly die from untreated bites and stings.

Let us take a look at those insects that bite, maul, sting, or make you sick in the wild:

1. **Mosquitoes**

Aside from the regular bugs and irritation caused by mosquitoes, it can also spread diseases like malaria, Zika, as as well as the Nile virus. They are mostly seen at night, and they also thrive in dirty places.

2. Bees and wasps

Bees and waps usually bite and sting. The resulting action leads to anaphylaxis which is easily identified by swelling of the lips and face, hives, fainting, and light headache.

3. Ticks

Here is another annoying insect found in the wild that transmits severe diseases like the Powassan virus and Lyme disease. A single tick bite can make you sick and needing medical treatment immediately.

4. Snakes

One common reptile that can attack people in the wild is known as snakes. They are proven to leave bite marks on humans that can kill instantly if medical treatment is not administered almost immediately.

A single snake bite takes about 6 minutes for the venom to spread around the body, causing damages to vital parts of the body and leading to death within a short period. The sad thing about snakes is that they are mostly found in the wild, and to keep yourself safe from the harmful effects of snake bites, it is important to always go with a wilderness first aid box.

5. Ants

Ants come in different species, and they vary depending on the region and surroundings. For example, the most dangerous type of ants is known to cause a severe allergic reaction like intense itching and anaphylaxis.

Unfortunately, ants are too little to spot, and you shouldn't be surprised to see them in your wilderness survival shelter housing because they need no permission to enter. With the most recommended wilderness first aid box, you can limit the allergic reaction caused by ant bites.

6. Fleas

These are also insects popularly known for causing bubonic plague, also known as the Black Death. This disease caused havoc in Europe in the middle ages.

Flea bites can cause severe allergies that can also cause serious itching of the skin. When moving to a wilderness spot, maybe for a particular task, try to study the common insects, animals, and reptiles present in that area. This will give you an idea of how to deal with bad situations and prepare your mind to solve any unforeseen circumstances that are likely to happen.

Wilderness First Aid Basics

Wilderness first aid is a significant skill that could be helpful in several survival situations. Albeit these methods were intended to be utilized outdoors, they can simply be applied in some other unforeseen circumstances. However, what is wilderness first aid?

Wilderness first aid can be characterized as the understanding and capacity to adequately react to and handle any sickness, injury, or outdoor emergency. These techniques are explicitly intended to work well even without modern facilities and tools and more modern gear.

A few wilderness first aid skills include:

- Treating burns and nibbles
- Setting injured limbs
- Dressing open injuries
- Controlling bleeding

In case of a mishap or backpack disaster, being equipped with the right skills and materials can go a long way in worsening injuries and saving lives.

The Basics

Preparation is the first and foremost step in any first aid treatment. Without the right materials and needed tools, it will be tough for you to recommend the right first aid items. Appropriate planning involves gathering an intensive and complete supply of things that are seen as first aid items like,

- Disinfectant
- Ointment to treat stings and bites
- Bandages
- Tweezers
- Benadryl

Before each trip, check your kit to know if any essential items need to be replaced or renewed. All your provisions ought to be perfect and in excess amount before leaving for the wilderness.

Obviously, having a complete kit of first aid materials and tools amounts to nothing if you don't know how to use them. Knowing everything about giving first aid, that is, identifying which supplies to use, when and how to utilize them, can make the difference between having a safe outdoor situation and a dangerous one.

First aid training is an important skill needed to thrive in the wilderness. You can attend first aid classes to equip yourself with all there is to know about administering first aid, especially if you want to spend most of your time in the wild.

Assuming you have just gone through past preparation but have forgotten some important things, there's no issue. You can simply enroll for supplementary classes in the following fields:

- Pediatric Advanced Life Support (PALS)
- Advanced Cardiac Life Support (ACLS)
- Basic Life Support (BLS)

General Safety

It's essential to ensure you can fend for yourself while out in the wild; however, ensure that, if you are in the wild with others, that they have your back. Ensure that somebody who will not climb or explore alongside you is aware of where you will be and has the means to reach you when things go wrong. Therefore, if things don't work out as expected, you can be rest assured that someone will help you get out of a bad situation.

Tying Basic Survival Knots

Tying knots is something you may have done for fun as a kid, but it can go a long way in saving your life. This section is detailed with five survival knots you should equip yourself with while venturing into the wild:

- Sheet bend
- Bowline knot
- Taut-line hitch
- Figure-eight knot
- Clove hitch

1. Sheet bend

If you want a long piece of rope, the sheet bend will permit you to tie the shorter pieces of rope with care. The sheet bend is effective even if the two strings do not have the same size or are made of diverse materials.

Sheet bend survival uses

- It is also an effective method of tying together multiple short strands of cord to create a cargo net without a long rope.
- Furthermore, cargo nets are suitable for building blocks in creating stretchers, fishnets, hammocks, and snowshoes.

Disadvantages

- The sheet bend is not a very rigid knot. This means it can lose if the rope is smooth or not enough force is applied to the knot.

Common mistakes and how to correct them

The most popular mistake in sheet bend is tying the sheet bend using the short end of a particular rope on the knot's wrong side. This is usually regarded as the "left-hand sheet ben." You can be sure of the knot by ensuring that the two free rope ends are on a similar knot side.

2. **Bowline knot**

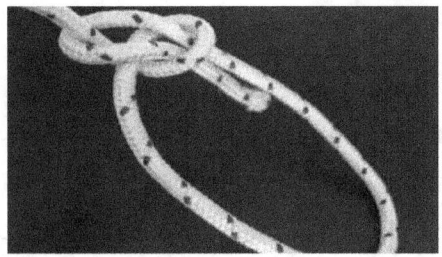

The bowline knot also retains thousands of pounds of force. The only difference between the bowline knot and the figure-eight knot is that the former is stress-free to unknot after use than the latter.

Furthermore, the bowline knot might be the most reliable of the entire survival knots that you must know.

Bowline survival uses

- The bowline knot can be wrapped around items and through items. Knowing how to tie the bowline knot with a single hand is an excellent skill that can help you when the situation calls for it.
- A bowline knot makes a loop at the edge of the rope, and the knot becomes very tight when force is applied to the loop. This is why it is vital for hanging materials from tree limbs such as survival gear and food.

Disadvantages

- You cannot depend on the bowline knot when climbing because mistakes are bound to happen.
- The knot can untie on its own if it is faced sideways.

Common mistakes and how to correct them

Due to the knot's untying likelihood, forming a stopper knot under the bowline knot will make it safer.

3. Taut-line hitch

The major advantage of using the taut-line hitch is that it can slide up and down the cord and tighten it. As a result, it keeps the rope taut and allows you to change the force applied. The hitch is easy to untie after it has been used.

Taut-line hitch survival uses

- It is used when taking shelter under a tarp.
- It permits your loop to slide and hold, making it easy to place in a large waterproof survival tarp.
- When making a buffer between you and others, stringing a rope between two trees and placing a tarp on its top is the initial step. However, to make a shelter out of the tarp, you must first get a tight rope to hang it from.

Disadvantages

- The taut-line hitch will not be effective for making a tight rope and keeping it that way.

Common mistakes and how to correct them

- Many people have a habit of tying the Magnus hitch, which is difficult to twist and is more likely to slip. To tie the best hitch, change the direction when tying the final half hitch.
- It is not tricky to accidentally change the rotation direction when tying the knot, making it weaker. However, you can be sure of this by ensuring the rope ends is in a similar direction.

4. Figure-eight knot

There are three significant kinds of figure-eight knots, and they include:

- Simple figure eight
- Figure-eight follow-through
- Figure eight on a bight

The simple figure-eight knot is the basic type of knot. It holds up to 85% of the rope's power, making it difficult to break while in use.

Figure-eight knot survival uses

- The figure-eight knot is used as a foothold when holding onto the rope becomes difficult due to harsh weather conditions.
- The figure-eight knot is also at the edge of the rope, which prevents you from sliding. It is a secure knot that cannot be untied due to force. Additionally, you can make knots along a rope that remains where it is and is large to hold when climbing.
- The figure-eight follow-through knot is the best kind of knot for climbing. This is because you can

create a safe loop at the edge of the rope with it. Another benefit is that it makes people feel safe.
- It is very vital for anchoring, especially in high wind situations.
- This knot on a bight forms a strong loop at the edge of the rope, making it able to hold onto an anchor. Individuals can further make stable loops in the center of the rope to work as footholds.

Disadvantages

- The major disadvantage of using the figure-eight knot is that it is usually tough to untie. This is because it has already been used multiple times. Furthermore, the knot also uses too much rope length, and it is not difficult to know if you have unintentionally tied it using the wrong method.

Common mistakes and how to correct them

The single major mistake you can make with the figure-eight knot is to include additional loops to the figure. This mistake is usually seen upon examination.

5. Clove hitch

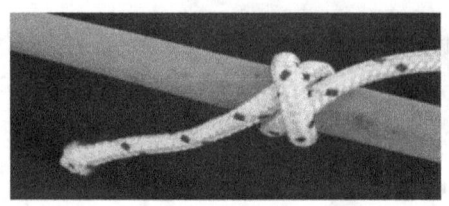

The clove hitch is known to be the knot that attaches a rope to an item or object. It is also an easy but vital survival knot that is straightforward and does not need any expertise to tie. The positive aspect you will receive from the clove hitch is that it does not slip or loosen easily, and you can make the rope long or short without interfering with the knot.

Clove hitch survival uses

- The clove hitch allows the rope to move without having to untie the knot. As a result, it effectively reduces heavy items or changes them to a much higher position.
- Also, a clove hitch is not strong compared to the bowline knot or figure-eight knot. However, it is a perfect know for anchoring, and it helps to fasten a shelter because it is always tight and does not loosen easily.

Disadvantages

Consistent movements such as the type triggered by a fierce and ferocious wind will surely make the knots loose, leading to an unbalanced shelter.

When this happens, you are expected to check the knots more often than not, which allows you to change them and tighten the loose parts.

Common mistakes and how to correct them

The clove hitch is very effective if there is enough force on the line. This is why it is a good option for keeping a tarp or a tent stretched. Endeavor not to utilize a clove hitch if the object it is tied to rotates because it is likely to become untied.

Yea, I know; I did not talk about how to make these knots; well, I have a well-detailed guide on how to make the above-mentioned knots and much more in my book *Knot Tying Book for Everyday Occasion* at https://www.amazon.com/dp/B08VLMR1VT

The end... almost!

Hey! We've made it to the final chapter of this book, and I hope you've enjoyed it so far.

If you have not done so yet, I would be incredibly thankful if you could take just a minute to leave a quick review on Amazon

Reviews are not easy to come by, and as an independent author with a little marketing budget, I rely on you, my readers, to leave a short review on Amazon.

Even if it is just a sentence or two!

So if you really enjoyed this book, please...

\>\> Click here to leave a brief review on Amazon.

I truly appreciate your effort to leave your review, as it truly makes a huge difference.

Chapter 5

Wilderness Survival Mistakes to Avoid

In this chapter, we have compiled the common survival mistakes you should aim to prevent if you ever want to thrive in the wild. Take a look at them below.

1. No decent navigation tools

Tragedy awaits those who travel into the wilderness without having a GPS, map, and compass. People who have stayed in the woods understand that one can lose his way in the bushes and thick trees within a few seconds.

The most important thing to know about navigating is to devise an alternative method to locate your way to safety. Do not rely solely on GPS because it is a machine that can most likely fail you.

Instead, you are expected to have a decent understanding of cardinal directions with the stars and sun because it also helps, especially if you find yourself in an unfortunate situation without proper preparation.

Here are a few tips to follow when navigating in the wilderness:

- Endeavor to take a compass and a physical map. Also, it is crucial to know how to operate them effectively.
- Use pace count beads to know how long a distance is.
- Understand what celestial bodies mean and how they are efficient for navigating.
- Research and study the map of the area before embarking on the journey. This will explain how the area looks like in case your compass or GPS fails you.
- Take an analog watch with you to know directions. Place the hour to point in the sun's direction and cross the distance between the minute and hour. The result will lead to the south path.

2. Lack of knowledge

Sadly, a high number of individuals in a wilderness survival situation have little or no knowledge of how to go about surviving. This is because they usually don't prepare for the worst before journeying into the wild.

Check out five essential knowledge for surviving in the wild:

1. **Learn how to build and sustain a fire:** Don't go into the wilderness without knowing how to make and maintain a lit fire.
2. **Learn how to make a shelter:** A shelter is vital for safety.
3. **Be acquainted with how to locate water and make it nontoxic to drink:** There are multiple ways to find water like rivers, lakes, morning dew, streams, ponds, melt snow, digging in damp soil, rainwater, and so much more. For the water to be safe for drinking, it has to be filtered via chemical extracts or boiling.
4. **Learn how to call for assistance:** Calling for help can be done using a flashlight, a fire, or a signal mirror.

5. **Learn what to eat and how to locate it:** Tons of food can be eaten in the wilderness without any side effects. We have covered this and above in the previous chapters, so you should go back to them.

3. Lack of shelter

Although this has been mentioned above, I need to re-emphasize this. Not having a place to stay in the wilderness can lead to your death if the situation becomes worse. Aside from not having a shelter, not being able to build one is more than dangerous for your survival.

Most people who have lost their lives in the wilderness were exposed to heatstroke or hypothermia. Make sure you don't leave your abode without going with the needed materials and tools for making a shelter.

Furthermore, items and materials like tarps, sleeping bags, cordage, tent, bivvies, and more should be taken along with you into the wilderness. We also discussed extensively on this in previous chapters.

Look below to see a few tips when building a shelter:

- The likes of grasses, vines, roots, and so on can work as the best option and serve as cordage for attaching poles.
- Utilize already fallen structures such as large rocks or fallen trees to build your shelter.
- Be extremely careful when adopting caves as a shelter. This is because you might not be the only animal around the wilderness.
- Do not build a shelter close to places where you can find dead standing trees or branches that are likely to fall.
- Build a lean-to rather than a complicated shelter. On the other hand, a lean-to does not retain heat, and it only protects you from a single direction.
- Don't lay on wet or cold grounds because it drains the body's heat rapidly.

4. Not Being Able to Find drinking water

To avoid situations where the body will be dehydrated, it is important to always drink water. However, where can one find nontoxic and good drinking water in the wilderness? Well, go through the previous chapters again, for this has been discussed extensively.

Bad water may contain waterborne organisms like giardia and cryptosporidium, leading to vomiting, severe diarrhea, and making you sick. Dehydration is also bad because it prevents you from carrying on in the woods.

Once you can find drinking water in the wilderness, you should purify it by adding chemical contents, boiling it, and adding water filters.

Check out a few tips for collecting water:

- Cover a plastic bag on a leaf tree and tie it. While this is ongoing, the leaves will release moisture inside the bag.
- Morning dew can be obtained using an absorbent material such as a cotton cloth on green leaves and pressed to remove the absorbed water.
- Some plant life can hold water that can be tapped and utilized.
- Look out for damp soil and dig it to get water.

Check out a few tips for making water clean:

- Create a field filter from a plastic bottle covered with rocks, charcoal, and sand.
- Dig a hole close to a water source and permit the water to enter through the underlying soil. The soil can serve as a filter and helps in isolating the dirt from the clean water.
- Clothing such as handkerchief, bandanna, and sock can separate dirt from clean water.

5. Unable to Start a Fire

Some examples of what fire means include:

- **Signal:** It is possible to sight a blazing fire burning far away at night and smoke when the sun is still out.
- **Warmth:** During the cold season, a stable fire can keep us warm.
- **Purifier:** Fire can be used to heat up and boil water for use.
- **Protection:** Fire can also be used to stay safe and prevent predators or any dangerous animal from coming close.

Tips for starting a fire:

- Some tools for starting a fire may include matches, magnesium rod, lighter, and friction methods.
- Don't enter the wilderness without having the right kit for creating fire. At the very least, go with matches and a lighter.
- Tinder includes the driest and fibrous material that is very receptive to flame or spark. Furthermore, kindling is a piece of stick that is less thick than your finger. And fuel is whatever is more than kindling.

6. Bad choice of clothes

Endeavor to always dress one layer warmer than what you require. While walking through the wilderness and feeling hot, you can always remove your clothes and tie them around your waist.

Additionally, always make sure you wear clothes that hold their warmth even after water gets hold of it. Get a shell jacket and pants of some type of snow and rain. Recall that hypothermia occurs at a temperature of more than 40 degrees F.

Some useful tips for clothing

- Always move along with a backup set of clothes that are kept in a waterproof container.
- Layer clothes that contain flannel, softshell jacket, hard-shell coat, wool, and synthetics should be worn.
- Endeavor to dress in three different layers, including a base layer, outer layer, and mid-layer.
- In cold situations, always dress in synthetics and wool. This is because they protect and aid to wick moisture off from the body, unlike cotton with no insulating property, i.e., absorbs moisture.

7. Underestimating the risk involved

A majority of wilderness survival situations begin so innocently. However, as time goes on, things or situations may turn out very wrong, and you may end up with a life and death situation.

Before hitting the wilderness, the best thing to do is to prepare for the worst situation even though you are unsure of what to expect. Ensure you take some time and draft a plan in case a worse situation happens.

Remember that failure to make a plan before you leave can be a tragedy. Look below for a few tips that will help you make a plan before going into the woods:

- Inform your neighbors, friends, and family members of your trip into the wild and tell them to search for you if you fail to show up at the stipulated time.
- Draft a list of the entire items you will most likely need during your trip.
- Pack the complete tools and materials needed to make your trip into the wilderness a smooth and enjoyable one. Regretting to take a particular material or tool can put you in a panic situation.
- Think about the **"what if"** situations and provide adequate and sufficient answers to them.

8. Lack of signal arrangement

Signaling for help or assistance when in trouble is an essential skill in wilderness survival situations. If you visit virtually every outdoor store, you will always find an area where signal options are made available.

The popular type of signal tools includes signal mirrors and whistles. However, you need to also equip yourself with the knowledge of how to start a fire.

Added necessary signal tools might include shiny wears, radios, flashlights, emergency beacon devices like SPOT and ACR. Meanwhile, if you are without any signal tool and find yourself in a bad situation in the wilderness, you can use any emergency signal tool like snow, trees, or even rocks.

Check out the outlined instructions for signaling for help in bad situations:

- Straight lines are not so common in nature, so making one with natural tools like a line in the snow may attract passersby's attention.
- Signal fire can be created quickly, and it has proven to be one of the most effective methods of calling for help. An intense fire can be spotted from far and while in the wilderness at night, it is inevitable that someone will answer your distress call.

Conclusion

Along with other outdoor activities, bushcraft is best taught and learned under the watch of experienced and knowledgeable survivalists. This book, however, aims to prep your mind on what you need to know to get started.

Bushcraft offers you the opportunity to live in the wild and thrive irrespective of unforeseen circumstances you encounter. But for this to happen, you need to have a survival mindset to push you through the wild and put you in a winning position. Although it requires a great deal of time to practice and master the art of surviving in an outdoor situation like in the woods, it is still worth the time and effort because no knowledge is wasted.

So then, get busy today by practicing all or most of what has been discussed in the pages of this book in a simulated-bushcraft location before hitting the woods; I believe this book will serve you very well enough to survive in the wild.

I wish you all the best

www.ingramcontent.com/pod-product-compliance
Lightning Source LLC
Chambersburg PA
CBHW050325120526
44592CB00014B/2057